Jazz Piano Masterclass

WITH

MARK LEVINE

THE DROP 2 BOOK

Includes CD

© 2006 SHER MUSIC CO., P.O. Box 445, Petaluma, CA 94953
All Rights Reserved. International Copyright Secured. Made in the USA.
ISBN 1-883217-47-4
Cover Art by Robert L Mulder, Dallas, Oregon
Graphic Design by Attila Nagy, Cotati, California
Finale Editor: Chuck Gee, San Francisco, California
Text Editor: Deborah Craig, Berkeley, California
CD Recorded at Morrison Center Recital Hall, Boise State University, Boise, Idaho
CD Audio Engineering by John Franzen

Dedication

To my teachers, who shaped and directed my musical experience in profound ways: Joe Pace, Munn Ware, Jaki Byard, Hall Overton, Herb Pomeroy, and Barry Harris.

Acknowledgments

THANK YOU…

Chuck Sher, for your vision and your support.

Chuck Gee, for your good cheer, good advice, and knowledge of Finale.

Deborah Craig, for being a whiz at the English language, and a great friend.

Larry Dunlap, for your eagle eyes.

John Franzen, for careful recording.

Murray Low and Dave Matthews, for your many valuable suggestions.

Robert Mulder, for your artwork.

Attila Nagy, for the cover design and formatting of the book.

Table of Contents

About the Author

I grew up in Concord, New Hampshire – not exactly the jazz capital of the world. I started studying piano when I was five, trombone at nine, and was emphatically not a prodigy on either instrument. When I was twelve, my brother Earl, six years older and in his first year of college, started bringing home jazz records.

I fell in love with Benny Goodman's 1938 Carnegie Hall recording, and quickly decided that music was going to be my future. Benny Goodman was soon followed by Shorty Rogers, and then Stan Kenton's "Artistry In Rhythm." A month or two after Stan, Earl brought home a Charlie Parker record, which I HATED.

A year later, my Dad retired and the family moved to Daytona Beach, Florida. I was very fortunate that retired New York jazz pianist Joe Pace lived there; he introduced me to the beauties of the II-V-I progression. By now, Bird's music was the only thing I wanted to play. My trombone education continued, thanks to another retired jazz musician, Chicagoan Munn Ware.

I attended Boston University, but rather than going to class, I hung out at Berklee School of Music most of the time. Nights found me standing in the alley next to the legendary club The Stables, checking out local heavyweights such as Jimmy Zitano, Jimmy Mosher, and the great Jaki Byard, with whom I was studying.

After graduating, I moved to New York for two years, studying with Hall Overton. I then moved back to Boston for another four years, where I studied privately with Herb Pomeroy.

One night, saxophonist Bob Porcelli, who played with Tito Puente and Mongo Santamaria for many years, took me to the Palladium to hear Puente playing opposite Tito Rodriguez. That's when my romance with la musica Latina began. I caught a break when the only Latin band in Boston at the time, named (I am not making this up), "Los Muchachos," called me. The leader was a great saxophonist named Dick "Taco" Meza, who went on to play in New York for many years with Tito Rodriguez, Tito Puente, and Tipica 73. The band also included Gene Perla, who became Elvin Jones' bassist, and super percussionist Don Alias. For the next month, Taco and Don played me Eddie Palmieri records and taught me how to play montunos.

I also made my first recording around this time, playing trombone on Houston Person's album, *Underground Soul,*[1] which sold about seven copies.

Los Muchachos broke up: Taco, Gene, and Don moved to New York; and I moved west to Los Angeles. I co-led a Latin jazz band there with Carmelo Garcia, whose personnel at various times included Luis Gasca, Richie Barrientos, George Bohannon, Wayne Henderson, Jerry Rusch, and Pete Christlieb.

I spent some time on the road with Mongo Santamaria, with whom I recorded *African American Latin.* Columbia Records released it 31 years later. For a couple of years, I played with Willie Bobo, one of my two favorite bandleaders (the other is Blue Mitchell).

Trumpet player Luis Gasca started bringing me up to San Francisco for gigs, and I realized that I was living in the wrong part of California. After moving to San Francisco, I played with Woody Shaw for two years. Also, I gigged with Joe Henderson, Blue Mitchell, and Harold Land. I recorded one CD with Joe Henderson, *Canyon Lady,* and one with Blue, *Blue Mitchell Live.* I also played and recorded several albums with, Cal Tjader, one of which, *La Onda Va Bien,* won a Grammy for Best Latin Album.

I wrote *The Jazz Piano Book* in 1990, and *The Jazz Theory Book* in 1995. In 1996 I went to Cuba with saxophonist Ron Stallings, where I studied with the great Cuban pianist Hilario Duran, who now teaches at Humber College in Toronto.

The Cuban trip led Ron and myself to form *Que Calor,* a Latin jazz band that shone brightly in the late 1990s. A couple of years later I formed *The Latin Tinge,* and we made three recordings, last of which, *Isla,* was nominated for a Grammy in 2003. (We lost, but I can forever refer to myself as "Mark Levine, Grammy Loser" ☺).

I now divide my time between the San Francisco Bay Area, where I play gigs and teach at The San Francisco Conservatory of Music and The Jazzschool, in Berkeley, and my cabin in the mountains near Boise, Idaho, where I mostly sit on my deck looking at the mountains, and practice my gimbri, a Moroccan instrument that I took up a couple of years ago.

---

1 Prestige Records.

Author, Mark Levine

Drop 2 is a method of voicing melodies for four voices – four trumpets, four saxes, four trombones, four voices, four of anything. This book is about its use by jazz pianists.

You need to know at least a little jazz harmony to make sense of this book: chord construction (the notes that make up a given chord), and the II-V-I progression. If you are a beginning jazz pianist, I suggest that you purchase a good jazz piano instruction book, and naturally, I recommend my own book.[2]

The accompanying CD has recordings of each example. The CD's track number is shown both in the text and in the printed music examples. I highly recommend listening to them as you go through the book!

Getting into the world of drop 2 requires learning some scales, and you'll start with the bebop major scale.

THE BEBOP MAJOR SCALE

Bebop scales are scales with an added chromatic passing note. With the little finger of your right hand, play **Ex. 1-3 (track #3)**, a scale known as the *bebop major scale*.[3] This is the C major scale with a *chromatic passing note,* G♯ (marked "cpn"), between the fifth and sixth notes of the scale. Play the scale again, this time both ascending and descending, with the little finger of your right hand.

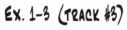

Ex. 1-3 (TRACK #3)

cpn

C BEBOP MAJOR SCALE

---

2   *The Jazz Piano Book,* Sher Music.
3   To further explore the bebop scales, see David Baker's many books on the subject, all available at www.jazzbooks.com.

Play **Ex. 1-1 (track #1)**, the first four bars of Kenny Dorham's "Blue Bossa."[1] This is the sound of drop 2.

Ex. 1-1 (track #1) Kenny Dorham's "Blue Bossa"

Play **Ex. 1-2 (track #2)**, the same four bars of "Blue Bossa," this time with drop 2 tweaked a bit, to make it sound more interesting.

Ex. 1-2 (track #2) Kenny Dorham's "Blue Bossa"

This book covers both the basic version of drop 2, demonstrated in **Ex. 1-1** and the more advanced version shown in **Ex. 1-2**.

1 Joe Henderson, *Page One*, Blue Note.

4-WAY CLOSE

You used your little finger to play the scale so you can use your other fingers to fill out the chords underneath, as shown in **Ex. 1-4 (track #4)**. Play this scale – now voiced – again both ascending and descending. Professional arrangers call this style of arranging *4-way close* because the four notes of each chord are bunched closely together.[4]

Ex. 1-4 (TRACK #4)

C BEBOP MAJOR SCALE IN 4-WAY CLOSE

You might recognize a similarity (especially if you're from the Midwest) between 4-way close and an old American music form, the barbershop quartet, most of whose harmonies are in 4-way close. Barbershop quartet harmony thus has been an unacknowledged influence on jazz, much like John Phillip Sousa (more on this when we get to **Ex. 1-26**).

---

4   Although this is a piano book, all these techniques are applicable to arranging for four voices, such as trumpet, trombone, and saxophone sections in bands, as well as four-voice vocal ensembles.

Notice that *Ex. 1-4* includes only two chords, C6 and a diminished 7th chord,[5] both shown in **Ex. 1-5 (track #5).** The C6 chord appears in root position, as well as all of its inversions, as shown in **Ex. 1-6 (track #6).** The same goes for the diminished chord shown in **Ex. 1-7 (track #7).**

Ex. 1-5 (track #5)

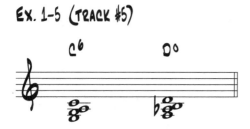

Ex. 1-6 (track #6)

Ex. 1-7 (track #7)

---

5 In the basic form of a diminished 7th chord, all the notes are a minor 3rd apart from the next closest note in the chord.

Alternating C6 and diminished chords sound so smooth because diminished chords are really *disguised V7♭9 chords* leading into the following chord. The effect is hearing a series of alternating I and V chords (C6 and G7♭9), as shown in **Ex. 1-8 (track #8)**. The diminished chord just happens to be the 3rd, 5th, 7th, and ♭9 of a G7♭9 chord, as shown in **Ex. 1-9 (track #9)**. Diminished chords as used in drop 2 are all disguised V7♭9 chords.

Ex. 1-8 (TRACK #8)   C BEBOP MAJOR SCALE AS I-V-I-V-I ETC.

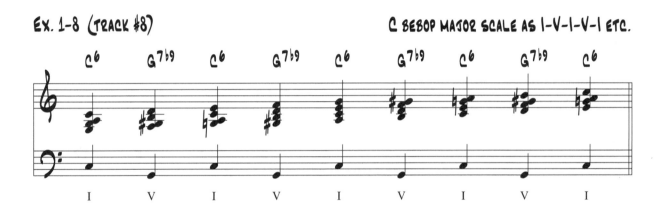

Ex. 1-9 (TRACK #9)

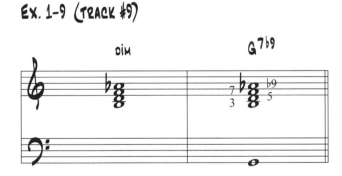

4-way close may sound great for four saxes, four trumpets, four trombones, four voices, and so on, but uses only a tiny fraction of the huge instrument at which you are sitting. George Shearing, an important pianist who arrived on the jazz scene in the '50s, developed a way of making 4-way close sound fuller by doubling the melody an octave below, playing the extra note with the left hand.[6] **Ex. 1-10 (track #10)** shows the C bebop major scale played in "Shearing Style."[7] Play it both ascending and descending.

Ex. 1-10 (track #10)

C bebop major scale in Shearing style

---

6 Many sources credit Milt Buckner, a jazz organist who came along ten years or so before Shearing, with inventing the style, often called "locked hands."

7 A great solo using Shearing style is Phineas Newborn, Jr.'s version of "On Green Dolphin Street," on his recording *"Back Home,"* Contemporary Records, 1976. Phineas' entry into Shearing-land starts at 3:10 of track #2.

DROP 2

Drop 2, the subject of this book, is more pianistic than Shearing style, because it uses more of the piano's range. **Ex. 1-11 (track #11)** shows our original C bebop major scale, this time voiced in drop 2. Here's what you do: Play the C6 chord in 4-way close (the first chord in **Ex. 1-4**). Take the second note from the top (A) out of the chord, drop it an octave, and play it with your left hand, as shown in **Ex. 1-12 (track #12)**. This is the sound of drop 2. Play the whole scale again, ascending and descending.

Ex. 1-11 (TRACK #11)

C BEBOP MAJOR SCALE IN DROP 2

Ex. 1-12 (TRACK #12)

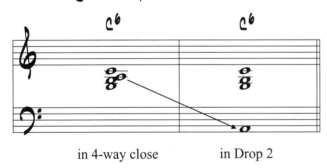

in 4-way close   in Drop 2

Ex. 1-13 (track #13) shows the technique applied to a diminished chord. First, play the chord in 4-way close; then play it with the second note from the top (B) dropped an octave into the left hand.

Ex. 1-13 (TRACK #13)

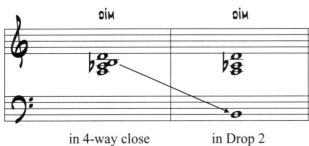

in 4-way close   in Drop 2

4-way close and drop 2 are great ways to voice melodies that follow a major scale. **Ex. 1-14 (track #14)** shows the first bar of Duke Ellington's "What Am I Here For?" in both 4-way close and drop 2. Note the relationship of the melody note to the chord (C6). When the melody is a chord tone (C and E), the chord is voiced as C6. When the melody note is a passing note (D, marked pn), the chord is voiced as a diminished chord. Duke's tune demonstrates a basic rule of both 4-way close and drop 2: *When voicing a melody on a major chord, voice chord tones as major 6 chords; voice passing notes as diminished chords.*[8]

Ex. 1-14 (track #14) Duke Ellington's "What Am I Here For?"

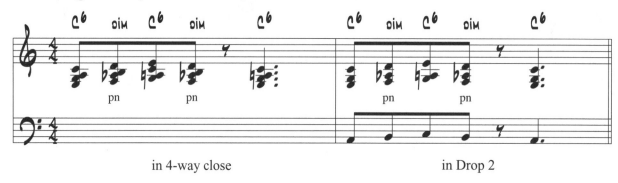

in 4-way close   in Drop 2

In the tune fragment shown in **Ex. 1-14**, C (the root), and E (the 3rd) are two of the *chord tones* of C6, as shown in **Ex. 1-15 (track #15)**. They are therefore voiced as C6 chords. The D, because it isn't the root, 3rd, 5th, or 6th, is a *passing note*. Because of this, it is voiced as a diminished chord.[9]

Ex. 1-15 (track #15)

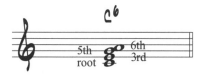

---

8 A good definition of *passing note* would be "a note from the implied harmony that is not a chord tone." D is the 9th of a C∆ chord. It is from the key of C, but it is neither the root, 3rd, 5th, or 7th of the chord. It is a passing note.

9 Chord tones" are the root, 3rd, 5th, and 7th (sometimes 6th) of a chord. A note that belongs to the scale of the chord, but is not a chord tone, can be called both a non-chord tone and a passing note.

Notice that I said "fragment" in the above paragraph. Its rare to play an entire tune in drop 2. Drop 2 sounds best in melodies with passages that move scale-wise (everything from "Mary Had A Little Lamb" to "Blue Bossa"). Drop 2 is very effective at the beginning of a tune, but you can "drop" drop 2 voicings anywhere in a song, or when soloing, even for a single chord.

Ex. 1-16 (track #16) shows the first four bars of Irving Berlin's classic "Always." Every note is a chord tone of A♭6, except for the B♭ (the 9th), which is voiced as a diminished chord, as shown in 4-way close – **Ex. 1-17 (track #17)** – and in drop 2 – (**Ex. 1-18 (track #18)**).

Ex. 1-16 (track #16)   Irving Berlin's "Always"

Ex. 1-17 (track #17)   Irving Berlin's "Always" in 4-way close

Ex. 1-18 (track #18)   Irving Berlin's "Always" in Drop 2

You may be wondering why all the major chords are major 6th chords. It's true that most major chords played in jazz are major 7th chords. But in the basic form of drop 2, major chords are major 6th chords. There is a way to convert major 6th chords into major 7th chords. We'll get to that in Chapter 2.

THE BEBOP MINOR SCALE

With the little finger of your right hand, play **Ex. 1-19 (track #19)**, the A bebop natural minor scale. The A bebop natural minor scale, starts on A, and the C bebop major scale shown just below it starts on C, but they both have the same notes. The two scales – C bebop major, and A bebop natural minor – have exactly the same intervallic relationship as do major and relative minor keys: the natural minor is a minor third below the major. Note that the chromatic passing note (G♯) is the same in both scales, except that it occurs between the seventh and eighth notes in the bebop natural minor scale, and between the fifth and sixth notes of the bebop major scale.

Ex. 1-19 (track #19)

Ex. 1-20 (track #20) shows the A bebop natural minor scale in 4-way close.

Ex. 1-20 (track #20)

A BEBOP NATURAL MINOR SCALE IN 4-WAY CLOSE

Ex. 1-21 (track #21) shows the A bebop natural minor scale in drop 2.

Ex. 1-21 (track #21)

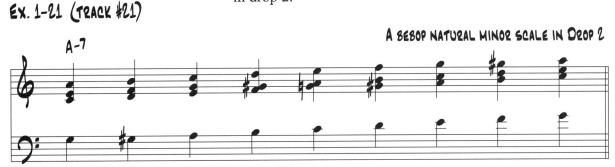

A BEBOP NATURAL MINOR SCALE IN DROP 2

As an example of the bebop natural minor scale, **Ex. 1-22 (track #22)** shows the first few bars of George Gershwin's classic "Summertime" in 4-way close. Note that most of the melody notes are chord tones – the root, 3rd, 5th and 7th of the A-7 chord. They are all voiced as A-7 chords. The two Ds in the melody are marked "pn" (passing notes), and are voiced as the same diminished chord. Note that the notes of the diminished chord are, reading from the bottom up, F, G#, B, and D – the 3rd, 5th, 7th, and ♭9 of E7♭9, the dominant chord resolving to A-7, the first chord of "Summertime."

Ex. 1-22 (track #22)   George Gershwin's "Summertime" in 4-way close

Ex. 1-23 (track #23) shows the same few bars in drop 2.

Ex. 1-23 (track #23) George Gershwin's "Summertime" in Drop 2

THE BEBOP DOMINANT SCALE

With the little finger of your right hand, play the scale in **Ex. 1-24 (track #24)**, the C bebop dominant scale. If you're familiar with jazz harmony, this is the same as the scale known as the C Mixolydian mode, except that it has a chromatic passing note – B natural – between the seventh and final note of the scale.

Ex. 1-24 (track #24)

Ex. 1-25 (track #25) shows the C bebop dominant scale in 4-way close.

Ex. 1-25 (track #25)

Ex. 1-26 (track #26) shows the C bebop dominant scale in drop 2.

Ex. 1-26 (track #26)

C BEBOP DOMINANT SCALE IN DROP 2

Ex. 1-27 (track #27) shows the four diminished chords that occur in the C bebop dominant scale. Note that one of them is different from the others. The first, second, and fourth diminished chords are the same chord – F, A♭, B, D – in different inversions. The notes in the third diminished chord are completely different – C, E♭, F♯, and A. It is nothing to worry about, but something that you should notice.

Ex. 1-27 (track #27)

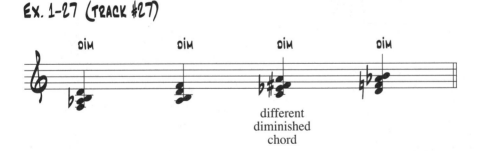

different
diminished
chord

Remember the earlier reference to John Phillip Sousa above? Play the C bebop dominant scale *descending*. These are the same nine notes that Sousa used as an introduction to many of his marches. If you've ever played in a marching band, you'll recognize it. Sousa was another of those surprising influences on early jazz that go unmentioned in jazz history books. Far-fetched? Not at all. Turn of the century New Orleans jazz bands were largely *brass* bands. Among other styles, they played marches, and Sousa, who lived at the same time, wrote marches.

McCoy Tyner, soundcheck for Spoleto Festival, Charleston, South Carolina, 1983

VOICING TUNES IN DROP 2

The basic rules for voicing melodies in drop 2 are simple:

1) Voice chord tones as major, minor, or dominant chords

2) Voice passing notes as diminished chords.

A definition of *chord tones* bears repeating: The chord tones of a major chord (and some minor chords) are the root, 3rd, 5th, and 6th or 7th, as shown in **Ex. 1-28 (track #28)**. The chord tones of a minor 7th chord are the root, 3rd, 5th and 7th, as shown in **Ex. 1-29 (track #29)**.

Ex. 1-28 (TRACK #28)

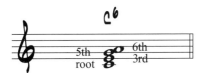

Ex. 1-29 (TRACK #29)

The chord tones of a dominant 7th chord are the root, 3rd, 5th and 7th, as shown in **Ex. 1-30 (track #30)**.

Ex. 1-30 (TRACK #30)

Now, check out the first few bars of Harry Warren and Mack Gordon's standard "There Will Never Be Another You," as shown in **Ex. 1-31 (track #31)**.

Ex. 1-31 (track #31) HARRY WARREN AND MACK GORDON'S "THERE WILL NEVER BE ANOTHER YOU"

Each melody note in **Ex. 1-31** is notated as either a chord tone or a passing note. Remember, chord tones are voiced as the root, 3rd, 5th, 6th of the chord symbol shown (E♭6 in this case), while passing notes (shown as pn) are voiced as diminished chords.

As you can see, most of the notes on the E♭6 chord are chord tones. The first two melody notes – B♭ and C – are the 5th and 6th of the E♭6 chord. The following note, D, is the major 7th of E♭6, not a chord tone (remember, in basic drop 2, major chords are *major 6* chords – major 7th chords will be covered in Chapter 2).

The next note, E♭, is the root, a chord tone. The last note in the first full bar is F, the 9th, a passing note. The next two notes – G and B♭ – are chord tones (the 3rd and 5th). Then F again, the 9th, a passing note, followed by E♭, the last melody note on the E♭6 chord, the root, a chord tone. Soon you'll learn how to voice the final note, F, which occurs on the chord in the last bar, Dø.

Again, *chord tones on major chords are voiced as major 6 chords; passing notes are voiced as diminished chords.*

Following these rules, **Ex. 1-32 (track #32)** shows these first few bars of "There Will Never Be Another You" in 4-way close. **Ex. 1-33 (track #33)** shows them in drop 2. The chord tones are voiced as E♭6, the passing notes as diminished chords.

Ex. 1-32 (track #32)
Harry Warren and Mack Gordon's "There Will Never Be Another You" in 4-way close

Ex. 1-33 (track #33)
Harry Warren and Mack Gordon's "There Will Never Be Another You" in Drop 2

Notice that the very first note, B♭ below middle C, is not voiced. The reason is a very important rule: *Notes below middle C are often too low to be voiced in drop 2.* That's not a hard-and-fast rule, just something to expect.

The final melody note in the fragment of "Another You," is an F, played on a D∅ chord. The symbol ∅ is often used to notate a half-diminished chord. *Half-diminished* is a fancy name for a simple chord: a minor 7th chord with a flatted 5th. The chord tones of a D∅ chord are D (the root), F (the 3rd), A♭ (the ♭5), and C (the 7th). The melody note F (the 3rd) is a chord tone.

Here are a few more fragments of tunes, voiced in drop 2:

The first four bars of Jerome Kern's "The Way You Look Tonight," as shown in **Ex. 1-34 (track #34)**.

Ex. 1-34 (track #34)   Jerome Kern's "The Way You Look Tonight" in Drop 2

Johnny Mandel's "The Shadow Of Your Smile," as shown in **Ex. 1-35 (track #35)**. There are two new chords in this example. E-6 and E-Δ are something new, *tonic minor* chords. You'll learn about them in Chapter 2.

Ex. 1-35 (track #35)   Johnny Mandel's "The Shadow Of Your Smile" in Drop 2

The first two bars of the bridge of Sigmund Romberg's "Lover Come Back To Me," are shown in **Ex. 1-36 (track #36)**. Again, here are some tonic minor chords.

Ex. 1-36 (track #36)   (Bridge of) Sigmund Romberg's "Lover Come Back To Me" in Drop 2

Most of the examples in this book are on the first few bars of various tunes. It is rare to be able to play drop 2 through an entire song. However, drop 2 combines well with other voicings. You might play a few bars of drop 2, then play left-hand voicings over a few bars, next play root position chords, and so on. Look for scale-wise motion in the melody; that's when drop 2 usually works best.

I recommend that you, the student, practice the scales in 4-way close and drop 2, until your ear, fingers, eyes and mind have absorbed what these new sounds hear, feel, and look like. Open your *New Real Book*[10] and read through as many tunes as you have time for, using drop 2 as often as possible. Once this approach works on a given tune fragment, your mind will remember the pattern you played, which should be easy to recall when you find the same melody or chord progression in another tune.

This chapter covered the basics. To get a more modern sound, you must learn how to tweak the chords to be more in tune with today's jazz.

Tweaking, means altering, adjusting, and improving on traditional drop 2, to obtain a more modern sound.

10 The *New Real Books*, from Sher Music Co., are the standard "fake" books used by most jazz musicians. See www.shermusic.com.

Kenny Barron, recording session, Systems Two Studio,
Brooklyn, New York, June 2003

The major chords we have used so far have all been major sixth chords, rather than the usual (in jazz harmony) major 7th chords. There are various ways to make major chords sound more modern when playing drop 2, and replacing the 6th with the major 7th is one of them. There are actually several "tweaks" to drop 2 major chords – tweaks that make the chords sound more modern, and plug you into the harmony of Bill Evans, Herbie Hancock, Barry Harris, Kenny Barron, McCoy Tyner, Chick Corea, and other jazz piano greats.

Ex. 2-1 (track #37), shows all four C6 chords in drop 2, as you played them in Chapter 1. The first one has the root in the melody, the second one the 3rd in the melody, the following one the 5th in the melody, the last one the 6th in the melody. Now take each of these chords and make them sound more modern.

Ex. 2-1 (track #37)   All four C6 chords in Drop 2

The four major chords shown in **Ex. 2-2a, 2-2b, 2-2c,** and **2-2d (track #38)**, show how changing one note can create a richer chord. The examples are each two bars: The bar on the left shows the traditional drop 2 version of the chord; the bar on the right shows the tweaked version, with one note raised or lowered.

EX. 2-2 (TRACK #38)   TWEAKING THE FOUR MAJOR CHORDS

EX. 2-2A

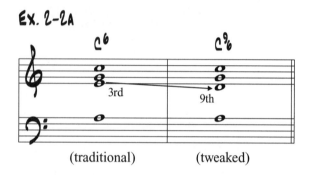

(traditional)   (tweaked)

EX. 2-2B

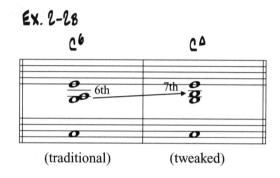

(traditional)   (tweaked)

EX. 2-2C

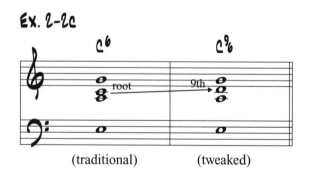

(traditional)   (tweaked)

EX. 2-2D

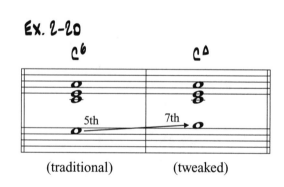

(traditional)   (tweaked)

Look at the first bar: the C6 chord with C (the root) in the melody. In the next bar, E, the 3rd of C6, has been dropped a whole step to D, the 9th. This creates a chord in which the notes are a perfect 4th away from each adjacent note. These *fourth chords* were first made popular by McCoy Tyner back in the early 1960s. The D in the voicing is the 9th of the chord, hence the chord symbol C6/9.

You may have noticed that the first chord in **Ex. 2-1** has been raised an octave in **Ex. 2-2a**. The chord in 4-way close sounds fine in **Ex. 2-1**, but will sound too muddy in drop 2. One of the things you have to learn about new voicings is the range in which they sound good on your own piano. What sounds great on a Hamburg Steinway might not sound quite so good on a Baldwin Acrosonic. If a chord sounds muddy or indistinct, it is too low.

Look at **Ex. 2-2b**, the C6 chord in the first bar has E (the 3rd) in the melody. In the following bar, the melody note A (the 6th) has been raised a whole step to B, the major 7th, creating a C major 7th chord, usually notated as CΔ.[11]

In **Ex. 2-2c**, the C6 chord in the first bar has G, the 5th, in the melody. In the second bar, C, the root, has been raised a whole step to D, the 9th, which yields another fourth chord.

In **Ex. 2-2d**, the C6 chord has A, the 6th, in the melody. G, the 5th, has been raised a major 3rd to B, the major 7th, creating another CΔ chord.

In each of these tweaks, anything in the chord above the 5th is shown in the chord symbol as the major 7th (notated as Δ), 6th, and/or 9th. If you were creating a lead sheet or piano part, you could notate all of these in, but jazz musicians often prefer simplicity and shorthand, so notating the numbers in the chord symbol is optional, or to the taste of the writer. CΔ would suffice for most of us.

---

11 Major 7th chords are notated in various ways: CMaj7; CMa7; CM7; and the more common CΔ, or even just "C."

Now play the C bebop major scale in drop 2 you played earlier in **Ex. 1-11,** and compare it to the tweaked version; both of them are shown in **Ex. 2-3 (track #39)**. Notice the difference? The second of the two scales sounds more modern, with the major 7th, 4th and 6/9 chords adding more color and intensity to the music. In addition, the diminished chords have been tweaked, an effect that will be explained soon in **Ex. 2-7.**

Ex. 2-3 (TRACK #39)

Ex. 2-4a (track #40) shows the first four bars of "Always"
as played in **Ex. 1-18. Ex. 2-4b** shows the same four bars,
but with all of the A♭ major chords (notated as either A♭6 or
A♭△) tweaked as just described.

Ex. 2-4 (track #40)

Ex. 2-4a   Irving Berlin's "always" in Drop 2

Ex. 2-4b   Irving Berlin's "always" tweaked

All notes above the 5th of the A♭ chord (6th, 6/9), are
notated in **Ex. 2-4b**. In real life, if you wrote out a lead
sheet or a piano part, you might choose to simply notate the
entire four bars as A♭△.

TWEAKING DOMINANT CHORDS

Ex. 2-5 (track #41) shows all four C7 chords in drop 2, as you played them in Chapter 1, in all four inversions, with the root, 3rd, 5th, and 7th in the melody.

Ex. 2-5 (track #41) ALL FOUR C7 CHORDS IN DROP 2

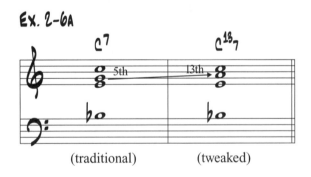

Ex. 2-6a, 2-6b, 2-6c, and **2-6d (track #42)** include the same four dominant chords as in **Ex. 2-5,** with a note or sometimes two notes changed (tweaked) in the next bar to create a richer chord. In **Ex. 2-6a** and **Ex. 2-6b,** G, the 5th, has been raised a whole step, becoming A, the 13th, in the following bars.

Ex. 2-6 (track #42) TWEAKING THE DOMINANT CHORDS

Ex. 2-6a

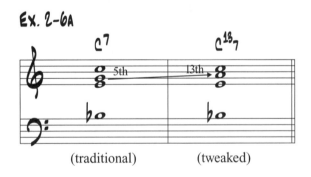

(traditional)   (tweaked)

Ex. 2-6B

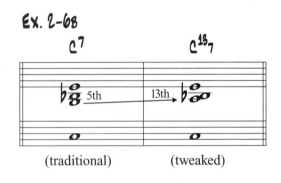

(traditional)   (tweaked)

Ex. 2-6c

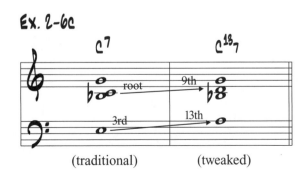

(traditional)   (tweaked)

Ex. 2-6D

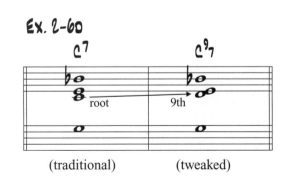

(traditional)   (tweaked)

In **Ex. 2-6c**, two notes have been tweaked. C, the root, has been raised a whole step to become D, the 9th. E, the 3rd, has been raised a fourth, to become A, the 13th.[12] In **Ex. 2-6d**, C, the root, has been raised a whole step, becoming D, the 9th, in the following bar.

In each of these tweaks, the new notes are shown in the chord symbol as 9 or 13. If you were writing out a lead sheet or piano part, you could notate them in the chord symbol, but jazz musicians prefer shorthand in chord symbols.

Most musicians will be happy with just "C7," and will color the chord with the 9th and/or the 13th as needed.

TWEAKING DIMINISHED CHORDS

The diminished chords that you have been playing sound a bit old-fashioned, sort of like the chords announcing the entrance of a silent movie villain.

Fortunately, it is easy to make diminished chords sound more modern. Just follow this rule:
In drop 2, *you can raise either the second or third note from the top in a diminished chord by a whole step.*

---

12 You might think "Wait a minute! A dominant 7th chord needs both a 3rd and a 7th." This is true much of the time, but is not an infallible rule. This chord sounds good even without the 3rd.

Play **Ex. 2-7 (track #43)**. The first bar is the same as the bebop dominant scale that you played in **Ex. 1-26**. In the second bar, the C7 chords have been tweaked with the addition of 9ths and 13ths, and each diminished chord has either the second or third note from the top raised a whole step.

The first three diminished chords (tweaked) in the second bar of **Ex. 2-7** have had the third note from the top raised. The final diminished chord has the second note from the top raised a whole step. Why not raise all of the second notes a whole step? Why not raise the third note? Why not some other combination? The reason is that they all work. It's a matter of individual taste, and I like the sound of this version best.

Try different combinations, as in **Ex. 2-8 (track #44)**. Do you like this version better? Try different combinations and choose the ones you like best.

TWEAKING MINOR CHORDS

There are two types of minor chords, defined by their function.

   1) a minor 7th chord that is part of a II-V progression is called a *II chord*. D-7 is a II chord when followed by G7, the V chord in the same key. The two chords form the D-7 G7 progression, the II-V progression in the key of C.[13]

   2) a minor 7th chord that is not part of a II-V progression is a *tonic minor* chord, also known as a *minor I* chord. D-7 followed by any chord other than G7 is often reharmonized as D-6 or D-Δ. II chords are minor 7th chords; V chords are dominant 7th chords. Tonic minor chords are I chords.[14]

---

13 An exception is when the II chord is followed by a tritone substitution of the V chord, as in D-7, D♭7. This still sounds and functions as a II-V.

14 Many musicians denote a tonic minor chord by using lower case Latin, as in "i". A II-V-I in minor is often notated as ii-V7-i. Learning different ways of notating the same thing is a valuable skill.

Now play the first example in this book again, **Ex. 1-1**, shown here as **Ex. 2-9 (track #45)**. This is a correct way to play "Blue Bossa" in drop 2, but it's not the only way. Jazz musicians love to reharmonize. The first chord is shown as C-7. That indicates a II chord, which is usually followed by a V chord in the same key. In this case, C-7 would be followed by F7 – but it isn't. This means that it might sound better as a C-6 chord. The same is true for the F-7 chord in the third bar. It is not followed by B♭7, so it might sound better to play it as F-6. **Ex. 2-10 (track #46)** shows the first four bars of "Blue Bossa" with both minor 7th chords changed to minor 6th chords.

Ex. 2-9 (track #45) Kenny Dorham's "Blue Bossa"

Ex. 2-10 (track #46) Kenny Dorham's "Blue Bossa"

Another option for a tonic minor chord is to play it as a minor-major chord, which has a minor 3rd and major 7th, as shown in the C minor-major chord **Ex. 2-11 (track #47)**. Now play **Ex. 2-12 (track #48)**, the first chord in "Blue Bossa" is now a minor-major chord, and the diminished chords are tweaked.

Ex. 2-11 (track #47)

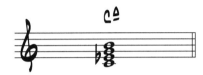

Ex. 2-12 (track #48) Kenny Dorham's "Blue Bossa"

Play **Ex. 2-12** a few times, and then go back and play **Ex. 2-9**. Which do you like best? **Ex. 2-12** is certainly much more radical than **Ex. 2-9**. If it's too far out for you, you don't have to tweak everything. By the way, **Ex. 2-9** and **Ex. 2-12** are the same as the first two examples at the beginning of the book, **Ex. 1-1** and **Ex. 1-2**.

C-Δ, the minor-major chord in **Ex. 2-12** was obtained by tweaking two notes of the original C- chord. **Ex. 2-13 (track #49)** shows how this was done. Both B♭, the minor 7th, and C, the root in the first chord have been moved up, to become B, the major 7th, and D, the 9th.

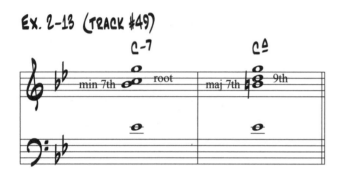

Ex. 2-13 (track #49)

Open your *New Real Books* and try voicing phrases of tunes in drop 2.
Look for songs with scale-like melodies. Here are a few suggestions:
Polka Dots And Moonbeams
Solar
Lullaby Of The Leaves
Softly, As In A Morning Sunrise
In My Solitude
In A Sentimental Mood
Someone To Watch Over Me

Now it's time to learn how to solo using drop 2.

Soloing and 'comping in drop 2 present both opportunities and problems. I'll show the opportunities first, and then discuss the problems.

ENCLOSURES

Enclosure means to precede a note with two other notes, one slightly above, the other slightly below.

Play **Ex. 3-1 (track #50)**, a simple descending melody outlining a C major triad containing the four notes G, E, C, G.

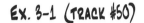

Ex. 3-2 (track #51) and **Ex. 3-3 (track #52)** show how you can enclose each melody note using drop 2.

In **Ex. 3-2** each melody note – G, E, C, G – is enclosed by two notes, one above the melody note and one below. These two notes can be either a half step or a whole step above or below the melody note, but to work in drop 2 *they must be a minor 3rd apart from each other, and must be from the same diminished chord.*

The first melody note in **Ex. 3-1** is G. The first note above and preceding G can be either G♯ or A. I'm choosing A in **Ex. 3-2**. A is part of the diminished chord that includes (reading down) A, F♯, E♭, and C. The second note below and following G has to be F♯, a minor 3rd down from A.

The second melody note in **Ex. 3-1** is E. In **Ex. 3-1** I'm preceding it with F, the note a half step above it. F's diminished chord is (reading down) F, D, B, and A♭. The next enclosure note will be D, a minor 3rd down from the first note, and from the same diminished chord.

I take the same approach on the next two melody notes in **Ex. 3-1**, C and G. C is enclosed with D and B. G is enclosed by A and F♯.

Ex. 3-3 shows **Ex. 3-2** played in drop 2.

Ex. 3-3 (TRACK #52)

Ex. 3-3 is fairly easy to play at a moderate tempo, but requires terrific chops to play at a fast tempo. The solution is to omit the two middle notes on the second chord of each enclosure, as shown in **Ex. 3-4 (track #53)**.

Ex. 3-4 (TRACK #53)

Ex. 3-5 (track #54) encloses almost the same melody as
in **Ex. 3-1**, but over a C-6 chord. The notes "enclosing" the
melody are from the same diminished chord – A♭, F, D, B.

Ex. 3-5 (track #54)

Ex. 3-6 (track #55) shows **Ex. 3-5** in drop 2.

Ex. 3-6 (track #55)

Ex. 3-7 (track #56) shows **Ex. 3-6** with the two middle
notes on the second chord of each enclosure omitted.

Ex. 3-7 (track #56)

Ex. 3-8 (track #57) shows the first four bars of Jerome Kern's "All The Things You Are." I'm going to solo over this using drop 2. Jazz musicians seldom play the exact changes notated. We like to reharmonize as we go along to make the song more interesting. That's what I'm going to do on these four bars.

EX. 3-8 (TRACK #57)   JEROME KERN'S "ALL THE THINGS YOU ARE"

Remember from Chapter 2 that there are two kinds of minor chords: II chords and tonic minor chords. If a minor 7th chord does not form a II-V progression with the following chord (as in D-7, G7), the minor 7th chord is best reharmonized as a tonic minor 6th or minor-major chord. That's exactly what I have done in **Ex. 3-9 (track #58)**. The F-7 chord is not followed by a B♭7 chord, which would make it a II-V, so I've reharmonized it as F- for now. I can decide whether to play it as F-6 or F-Δ soon. The same goes for the B♭-7 chord. It is not followed by E♭7, so I have reharmonized it, for now, as B♭-.

EX. 3-9 (TRACK #58)   JEROME KERN'S "ALL THE THINGS YOU ARE"

I have reharmonized E♭7, the chord in the 3rd bar of **Ex. 3-9**, using *tritone substitution*.[15] I replaced the E♭7 chord with A7, the dominant chord a tritone away from E♭7. I then preceded A7 by its II chord to create a II-V progression, E-7 A7.

Ex. 3-10 (track #59)   Jerome Kern's "All The Things You Are"

Ex. 3-10 (track #59) shows a four-note lick that I might sequence[16] through the changes of these first few bars of the song while soloing. In the first bar, I have outlined the root, 3rd, and 5th, as shown in **Ex. 3-11 (track #60)**. I have reharmonized E♭7, the chord in the third bar, to E♭7alt, followed by A7. I have enclosed the A♭△ chord in **Ex. 3-10**.

Ex. 3-11 (track #60)

---

15 For a full explanation of tritone substitution, see *The Jazz Piano Book* and *The Jazz Theory Book*, Sher Music.

16 A sequence is a musical phrase repeated, but also reshaped to fit the changing harmony. Think of the first movement of Beethoven's Fifth Symphony. The familiar "da-da-da-daaaaa" is followed by another "da-da-da-daaaaa," but at a lower pitch, to accommodate the second chord.

Ex. 3-12 (track #61) is another example of improvising over the first four bars of "All The Things You Are."

Ex. 3-12 (TRACK #61)

Hold on! That's too challenging for most people. **Ex. 3-13 (track #62)** shows a rhythmically simplified version.

Ex. 3-13 (TRACK #62)

Ex. 3-13 on page 38, uses several techniques:

In bar #1:

1) The original F-7 chord has been reharmonized as F-6.
2) An improvised melody ascends the first three notes of the F bebop minor scale in drop 2.
3) The fourth chord in the bar is a diminished chord, but not from the F bebop minor scale indicated by the chord symbol F-6. It is a transitional chord, a dominant 7th chord inserted to flow smoothly into B♭-6, the following chord. Its four notes – A, C, E♭ and F♯ – are the 3rd, 5th, 7th, and ♭9 of F7♭9, the dominant chord that resolves to the next chord, B♭-6. These disguised F7♭9 chords are shown in parentheses.
4) The two diminished chords are tweaked, with the third note from the top raised a whole step.

In bar #2:

1) The original B♭-7 chord has been reharmonized as B♭-6.
2) The diminished chord has been tweaked, the third note from the top raised a whole step.

In bar #3:

1) The first three chords are all from the altered bebop minor scale, which we'll get to soon.

In bar #4:

1) The first three chords form an enclosure around A♭△, which isn't played until the "and of 3."
2) The A♭△ chord has been tweaked into a fourth chord.
3) Some notes in the enclosure have been omitted for ease of playing.

After you've played **Ex. 3-13** a few times, go back and tackle **Ex. 3-12.** It's more difficult, but the rhythms make it sound much better.

Ex. 3-14 (track #63) is almost the same **Ex. 3-12**, but with a crucial difference: *All the right hand notes are played staccato, while the left hand plays legato.* This brings out the bass line, a 10th away from the melody. Playing the right-hand notes staccato while the left hand is played legato brings out the melody line created by the bass. Listen carefully to this example on the accompanying CD.

Ex. 3-14 (Track #63)

Ex. 3-15 (track #64) shows an even better effect, this time with both the left hand sustained, the right hand staccato, *and* the right hand played softly, the left hand louder.

Ex. 3-15 (TRACK #64)

When playing drop 2, it's a good idea to play the left hand slightly louder than the right hand, to enhance the drop 2 effect.

Now play the same passage while using *both* effects.

To tackle those chords in bar three, you need to learn a new scale, called (for lack of any official name) the *altered bebop minor scale.*

Bill Evans

THE ALTERED BEBOP MINOR SCALE

Ex. 3-16 (track #65) shows the C altered bebop minor scale. This scale is different from the other scales you have studied because it doesn't routinely alternate a chord (major, minor, or dominant) with a diminished chord. Look at the 7th chord in the scale, which I labeled, somewhat arbitrarily, G7alt. Remember, in Chapter 1 (**Ex. 1-8** and **Ex. 1-9)**, I reduced everything to I and V chords, with *all diminished chords being disguised V7♭9 chords.* **Ex. 3-17 (track #66)** shows a sequence of I-V-I-V-I-V-V-V-I. Those three V chords in a row create possibilities.

Counting from the beginning of **Ex. 3-17,** look at the sixth and seventh chords in the bar, notated "dim" and "G7alt." The "dim" chord is also G7♭9 (remember, all diminished chords in drop 2 are disguised V7♭9 chords). The "G7alt" chord is arbitrarily named; it is an unusual voicing for an alt chord and other pianists might notate it as something else.

Ex. 3-18 (track #67) starts with these two chords, and then repeats them a minor 3rd up, a minor 3rd up again, and so on, following the whole-step, half-step diminished scale.

Ex. 3-18 (TRACK #67)   TWO CHORDS ASCENDING IN MINOR 3RDS

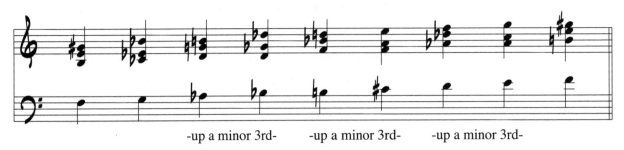

-up a minor 3rd-   -up a minor 3rd-   -up a minor 3rd-

Many improvised lines follow this whole-step/half-step pattern. **Ex. 3-19 (track #68)** shows the line over a *minor II-V progression.*[17]

Ex. 3-19 (TRACK #68)

Remember, all diminished chords in drop 2 are disguised V7♭9 chords.

---

17 A minor II-V is a II-V progression in which the II chord has a ♭5 (as in Dø) and the V chord has a ♭9 or is an alt chord (as in G7♭9 or G7alt).

PROBLEMS WITH DROP 2

A word of caution about playing drop 2 while 'comping: It's best to play drop 2 when there is space in the solo, when the soloist takes a breath. Because so many of the enclosure notes may be from a different scale than what the soloist is playing, overdoing drop 2 can create problems. For instance, in **Ex. 3-3**, a horn player may be improvising on the melody by playing in the C major scale, which the melody implies. If you're playing all those F♯s, E♭s and A♭s in the example, you might get a glare from the soloist, or he or she might call someone else for the next gig! Be judicious using drop 2 when 'comping. Develop radar that allows you to sense when the soloist is about to pause or breathe. Wynton Kelly was the acknowledged master of this skill, and I suggest that you listen to his recordings, especially the ones he did with Miles Davis.

Barry Harris

Practicing drop 2 can be a challenge. Your fingers aren't used to playing these four-note configurations, and your eye isn't used to seeing them either. To master this style *you must practice everything in every key,*

SCALES, CHORDS, ENCLOSURES, AND SOLO PATTERNS

In order to play drop 2 successfully, you will need a practice routine. What follows are some suggestions as to what you should be practicing.

SCALES

Ex. 4-1 (track # 69) shows the bebop major scale, both traditional and tweaked. Practice both versions in every key.

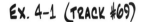

Ex. 4-2 (track #70) shows the bebop melodic minor scale, both traditional and tweaked.

EX. 4-2 (TRACK #70)

Ex. 4-3 (track #71) shows the bebop dominant scale, both traditional and tweaked.

EX. 4-3 (TRACK #71)

Ex. 4-4 (track #72) shows the bebop natural minor scale, both traditional and tweaked.

Ex. 4-4 (track #72)

Ex. 4-5 (track #73) shows the C altered bebop minor scale.

Ex. 4-5 (track #73)

CHORDS

Ex. 4-6 (track #74) shows the major chords, both traditional and tweaked.

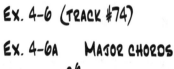

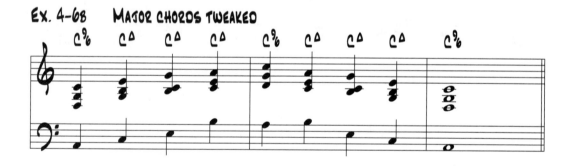

Ex. 4-7 (track #75) shows the tonic minor chords, both traditional and tweaked. Notice how some of the tweaked versions morph into minor-major chords,

EX. 4-7 (TRACK #75)

EX. 4-7A   TONIC MINOR CHORDS

EX. 4-7B   TONIC MINOR CHORDS TWEAKED

Ex. 4-8 (track #76) shows the dominant chords, both traditional and tweaked.

Ex. 4-8 (track #76)

Ex. 4-8a   Dominant chords

Ex. 4-8b   Dominant chords tweaked

Exs. **4-9a, 4-9b,** and **4-9c (track #77)** show the diminished chords, both traditional (**Ex. 4-9a**) and tweaked in two different ways (**Ex. 4-9b** and **Ex. 4-9c**), with the second note from the top raised a whole step and with the third note from the top raised a whole step. When playing these chords in real life, you can mix them in any way.

Ex. 4-9 (track #77)

Ex. 4-9a   Diminished chords

Ex. 4-9b   Diminished chords, 2nd note from top raised a whole step

Ex. 4-9c   Diminished chords, 3rd note from top raised a whole step

When playing diminished chords there are not twelve "keys". Everything repeats at the interval of a minor 3rd in diminished harmony.

1) The C diminished chord has the same notes as the E♭, F♯, and A diminished chords.

2) The C♯ diminished chord has the same notes as the E, G, and B♭ diminished chords.

3) The D diminished chord has the same notes as the F, A♭, and B diminished chords.

In other words there are only three "keys" in diminished harmony.

ENCLOSURES

Ex. 4-10 (track #78) shows a typical enclosure pattern on a major chord.

Ex. 4-11 (track #79) shows an enclosure pattern on a minor chord

Ex. 4-11 (track #79) Enclosure in minor

Start on different notes every time you practice. First enclose the 5th of the chord, as shown in the above two examples. Next, start with the 3rd, then the root, and then the 6th.

SOLO PATTERNS

To prepare yourself for soloing in drop 2, you need to diligently practice scale-like lines over familiar chord progressions. As you practice, your eyes gradually begin to "see" the harmony on the keyboard in a new way. The following patterns are not necessarily meant to be memorized and then played at your next jam session. Instead, their purpose is to acclimate you to a new way of playing, a new way of seeing the notes on the piano.

Ex. 4-12 (track #80) shows a five-note pattern played on a minor-major chord, and played *around the cycle of 5ths*. Because most music in real life follows the cycle, practicing using the cycle of 5ths is a must, as you want your practicing to be as close to real life as possible.[18]

Ex. 4-12 (track #80) Lick around the cycle of 5ths

18 Think of the roots of a II-V-I progression in C: D-7 G7 CΔ. The roots of the chords (D, G, C) follow counterclockwise around the cycle of 5ths.
Classical pianists take note: You probably already think of the cycle of 5ths as moving clockwise (C, G, D, etc.). Jazz musicians *always* use the cycle moving *counterclockwise* (C, F, B♭, etc.).

Ex. 4-13 (track #81) shows a line on a minor II-V progression.

Ex. 4-14 (track #82) shows a line walking up the bebop minor scale on a series of minor 6th chords around the cycle of 5ths.

Ex. 4-15 (track #83) shows a *chromatic approach* to a chord. The F-Δ chord is preceded by an F♯-Δ chord.

Take your favorite licks and scale-wise patterns and try revoicing them in drop 2.

SOME FINAL THOUGHTS ON DROP 2

Drop 2 isn't easy. It requires LOTS of practice, and in every key. Partly this is because it forces you to see the keyboard in a new way, voicing chords from the top down, rather then the traditional way from the bottom up. Seeing the same old 88 keys in a new way can be a revolutionary step in one's own musical growth.

I can't exaggerate the importance the way the keyboard *looks* in learning to play drop 2. The notes may change when going from a voicing on F♯ø to the same one on Dø, but the spaces between the notes remain the same. Learning to see the piano in this way greatly helps in mastering drop 2.

Good luck, and practice!

Cedar Walton

Glossary

II-V-I the basic chord progression played in jazz.

4-way close a four-note chord, the notes of which are voiced tightly together

bebop scales traditional scales – such as major, minor, Mixolydian, etc. – but with an added chromatic passing note

chord tones the root, 3rd, 5th, and 6th (or 7th) of a chord

chromatic approach preceding a note or a chord with another, a half step away.

chromatic passing note a note added between two scale tones a whole step apart (for example, G♯, in a scale that has a G and an A)

'comping accompanying, complimenting

cycle of 5ths the twelve notes of the chromatic scale organized in a series of descending 5ths

diminished chord a four-note chord in which every note is a minor 3rd away from the closest note in either direction

drop 2 4-way close, with the second note from the top dropped an octave (on piano, the dropped note is played with the left hand)

enclosure preceding a note with two notes, one above, the other below

fourth chord a chord in which all adjacent notes are a perfect 4th apart

half-diminished chord a minor 7th chord with a flatted 5th

inversion a chord in which the notes are rearranged so that the root is no longer on the bottom

locked hands an older term for the Shearing style, attributed to organist Milt Buckner

minor I *see* tonic minor

minor II-V progression a II-V progression in which the II chord has a ♭5, and the V chord has a ♭9 or is an alt chord

passing note a note in the scale implied by the chord symbol, but not a chord tone

Shearing style 4-way close with the melody doubled in the left hand

sixth-diminished what master jazz pianist Barry Harris calls drop 2

tonic minor a minor chord that functions as a tonic chord, also known as a minor I, rather than as the first chord in a II-V progression

tritone the interval of an augmented 4th, also known as a diminished 5th

tritone substitution substituting a dominant 7th chord with another dominant 7th chord whose root is a tritone away

tweak to alter, adjust, improve

Author, Mark Levine

Interview with Myself

I have enlisted the help of my evil twin, ET, to ask me the questions I've been waiting to be asked, to no avail, all my life.

ET: What's the worst question you've ever been asked by an interviewer?

ML: No question asked of myself tops the one I heard from a KRE disc jockey in Berkeley, after introducing McCoy Tyner to his listeners: "How come you sweat so much when you play?"

ET: Moving on...what got you interested in drop 2?

ML: I first studied it as an arranging technique with Herb Pomeroy, the harmony guru for many years at Berklee. I was aware that as a voicing technique it was used by piano players, but didn't follow up on it. Many years later I was listening to a Kenny Barron record and heard him play something in drop 2, and the light bulb went on. A bit later, I attended a clinic by Barry Harris, a master of drop 2,[19] and he filled in a lot of holes in my knowledge of the diminished chord.

ET: You seem to have a considerable interest in many genres – jazz, Cuban, North African – world music?

ML: Today, the term world music is used principally as a marketing tool, but I see it in very specific musical terms: find the crossing points and commonalities between genres, combine them, and create something new. For myself, that means jazz, Latin music, and African – particularly Moroccan – music. The commonalities include the pentatonic scale and two-bar rhythmic patterns, such as clave, found in most cultures. These two things are, for myself, the glue that holds the music together.

---

19 Barry calls drop 2 "sixth-diminished." Barry came up in Detroit in the '40s, and maybe that's what it was called there at the time.

ET: Are there any particular world music artists who inspire you?

ML: Nguyen Le, Hermeto Pascoal, Moacir Santos, Luis Perdomo, Dafnis Prieto, Nour-Eddine, Karim Ziad, and many others.

ET: Most Americans aren't familiar with any of these artists. Can you tell me a little about them?

ML: Nguyen Le[20] is a Vietnamese-French guitarist, composer, and arranger. That description doesn't do him justice, any more than does describing Hermeto[21] as a Brazilian accordion player. Both are renaissance figures, combining different genres in new ways. You have to hear their music to understand their importance. Elvis Costello once said, "writing about music is like dancing about architecture."

Moacir[22] was a Brazilian genius with whom I was lucky to work with. Ziad[23] is an Algerian drummer, composer, gimbri (a Moroccan lute) player, member of Joe Zawinul's band, and Nguyen Le's co-producer on two of their recordings. Pianist Luis Perdomo[24] and drummer Dafnis Prieto have erased the line between jazz and Cuban music. Nour-Eddine[25] is a Moroccan musician creating fusions of Moroccan Gnawa and Western music.

ET: How do you see yourself in this mix?

ML: I fell in love with the gimbri, the Moroccan instrument played in Gnawa music. I've been practicing it, and my next band will combine jazz, Cuban, Gnawa, and sundry other stuff. Or not. I'll be ready to play the gimbri in public in 25 years or so, but I may first have to move to Morocco. ☺

20 Nguyen Le, *Maghreb & Friends,* ACT Records; *Tales of Vietnam,* ACT Records.
21 Hermeto Pascoal, *Slaves Mass,* Warner Bros. Records.
22 Moacir Santos, *Saudade,* Blue Note Records; *Maestro,* Blue Note Records.
23 Karim Ziad, *Ifrikya,* ACT Records
24 John Benitez, *Descarga In New York,* Khaeon Records, features both Perdomo and Prieto.
25 Nour-Eddine, *Co-Exist,* Sconfini Records.

ET: What are your favorite pianos?

ML: I've been to heaven on a 7-foot Feurich, a 7-foot Bosendorfer, and a couple of 9-foot Hamburg Steinways. Because I haven't won the lottery yet, a Yamaha C-7 will have to suffice.

ET: And the worst one?

ML: In a bar in a small town in Italy – a Mitsubishi! I think it was made by their truck division.

ET: Your favorite keyboard?

ML: The Suitcase model Fender Rhodes.

ET: Who are the best bandleaders you've ever worked for?

ML: I'm glad you asked. Blue Mitchell, Willie Bobo, Woody Shaw, and Joe Henderson. They just let me play, without a lot of verbiage.

ET: Who was the most challenging bandleader you've worked for?

ML: David Liebman. The wildest rollercoaster ride of my life. You never knew what was going to happen next, or even what tune you're supposed to be playing. I just held on for dear life. Absolutely exhilarating.

ET: Lowest point in your career?

ML: I once lost a gig to Dweezil Zappa.

ET: Care to elaborate?

ML: No.

ET: You have traveled quite a bit in your career. Favorite countries?

ML: Cuba, for the music. Iceland, for the scenery.

ET: Did you ever play play pop or rock?

ML: For a couple of years in LA, I played in a top 40 band. It was a good time to be playing pop: Carole King, Stevie Wonder, James Taylor, etc.

ET: Your favorite pianists?

ML: Too many to list them all, but Tatum, Monk, Red, Wynton, Bill, Herbie, McCoy, Mulgrew, Luis Perdomo, Cedar, Peruchin, Kenny Barron….

ET: Most inspiring teachers?

ML: My first teacher, Joe Pace, a retired NY jazz pianist living in Daytona Beach, where I went to high school. He taught me about II-V-I. Jaki Byard taught me to just play, Herb Pomeroy taught me about harmony, Barry Harris taught me about drop 2, and Hall Overton introduced me to Monk's music.

ET: Earliest musical experience?

ML: I grew up in Concord NH, a small town with few opportunities to hear live music. My Mom took me to hear Perry Como, of all people, when I was about seven years old, and I decided that night to become a musician.

ET: Perry Como? Was it the cardigan?

ML: No.

ET: Heard anything new and exciting recently?

ML: I recently was in Peru, and heard an Afro-Peruvian band named Milenio that knocked me out.

ET: Strangest gig?

ML: With Bud Freeman, when I was 20 and he was about 80. I didn't have a clue what to play, but he was very encouraging. I wish I had brought a tape recorder with me that night.

ET: Any other times you wish you had had a tape recorder with you?

ML: Yes, when Lionel Hampton sat in with me.

ET: Sat in with your band?

ML: No, sat in with me. I was in Paris, and noticed that Hamp's band was playing at the Meridian Hotel. I knew Bob Bagard, his pianist, so I went by the hotel and gave him a ring. We went down to the ballroom, which was called the "The Lionel Hampton Room." We sat at the piano and showed each other stuff, with my friend's tape recorder on.

I was sitting at the piano and Hamp walked in. He got up on the bandstand, uncovered his vibes, and without any introduction, turned to me and asked "do you know 'Giant Steps'?" I said yes, he then played about 20 choruses, while I happily 'comped away and wondered if I was dreaming. Hamp arpeggiated 1-3-5-7 on every chord, up and down, up and down. I don't think he ever went beyond the 7th of any chord. Then he asked "do you know 'Moment's Notice'?" 20 more choruses. We stopped, he shook my hand, said "thank you," and walked out.

I turned to my friend and asked "what was that all about?" He said that Hamp wanted the band to sound more modern, and had commissioned someone to write charts on those two tunes. I said "wow!" and told him I wanted a copy of the tape. He said "oh, you wanted me to record that?" Arrgh.

ET: Funniest piano story?

ML: The late Al Plank, a wonderful Bay Area pianist, was playing solo piano at a San Francisco restaurant one night. A waiter walked up to him, handed him a dollar bill, and said "that diner over there would like you to play "Feelings" and "New York, New York." Al tore the dollar bill in half, handed half back to the waiter, and said "tell him I only know one of them."

ET: Anything else you'd like to add?

ML: No.

Index

Latin Music Books & CDs from Sher Music Co.

The Latin Real Book (C, Bb or Eb)

The only professional-level Latin fake book ever published! Over 570 pages. Includes detailed transcriptions of tunes, exactly as recorded by:

Ray Barretto	Irakere	Andy Narell	Ft. Apache Band	Djavan
Eddie Palmieri	Celia Cruz	Mario Bauza	Dave Valentin	Tom Jobim
Fania All-Stars	Arsenio Rodriguez	Dizzy Gilllespie	Paquito D'Rivera	Toninho Horta
Tito Puente	Tito Rodriguez	Mongo Santamaria	Clare Fischer	Joao Bosco
Ruben Blades	Orquesta Aragon	Manny Oquendo & Libre	Chick Corea	Milton Nascimento
Los Van Van	Beny Moré	Puerto Rico All-Stars	Sergio Mendes	Leila Pinheiro
NG La Banda	Cal Tjader	Issac Delgaldo	Ivan Lins	Gal Costa
				And Many More!

Muy Caliente!
Afro-Cuban Play-Along CD and Book
Rebeca Mauleón - Keyboard
Oscar Stagnaro - Bass
Orestes Vilató - Timbales
Carlos Caro - Bongos
Edgardo Cambon - Congas
Over 70 min. of smokin' Latin grooves! Stereo separation so you can eliminate the bass or piano. Play-along with a rhythm section featuring some of the top Afro-Cuban musicians in the world!

The Latin Real Book Sampler CD

12 of the greatest Latin Real Book tunes as played by the original artists: Tito Puente, Ray Barretto, Andy Narell, Puerto Rico Allstars, Bacacoto, etc.

$16 list price. Available in U.S.A. only.

101 Montunos
by Rebeca Mauleón

The only comprehensive study of Latin piano playing ever published.

- Bi-lingual text (English/Spanish)
- 2 CDs of the author demonstrating each montuno
- Covers over 100 years of Afro-Cuban styles, including the danzón, guaracha, mambo, merengue and songo—from Peruchin to Eddie Palmieri.

The True Cuban Bass
By Carlos Del Puerto, (bassist with Irakere) and Silvio Vergara, $22.

For acoustic or electric bass; English and Spanish text; Includes CDs of either historic Cuban recordings or Carlos playing each exercise; Many transcriptions of complete bass parts for tunes in different Cuban styles – the roots of Salsa.

The Brazilian Guitar Book
by Nelson Faria, one of Brazil's best new guitarists.

- Over 140 pages of comping patterns, transcriptions and chord melodies for samba, bossa, baião, etc.
- Complete chord voicings written out for each example.
- Comes with a CD of Nelson playing each example.
- The most complete Brazilian guitar method ever published! $28 list price.

Joe Diorio – "Nelson Faria's book is a welcome addition to the guitar literature. I'm sure those who work with this volume wiill benefit greatly"

The Salsa Guide Book
By Rebeca Mauleón

The only complete method book on salsa ever published! 260 pages. $25

Carlos Santana – "A true treasure of knowledge and information about Afro-Cuban music."
Mark Levine, author of The Jazz Piano Book. – "This is the book on salsa."
Sonny Bravo, pianist with Tito Puente – "This will be the salsa 'bible' for years to come."
Oscar Hernández, pianist with Rubén Blades – "An excellent and much needed resource."

The New Real Book Series

The Standards Real Book (C, Bb or Eb)

Alice In Wonderland
All Of You
Alone Together
At Last
Baltimore Oriole
A Beautiful Friendship
Bess, You Is My Woman
But Not For Me
Close Enough For Love
Crazy He Calls Me
Dancing In The Dark
Days Of Wine And Roses
Dreamsville
Easy To Love
Embraceable You

Falling In Love With Love
From This Moment On
Give Me The Simple Life
Have You Met Miss Jones?
Hey There
I Can't Get Started
I Concentrate On You
I Cover The Waterfront
I Love You
I Loves You Porgy
I Only Have Eyes For You
I Wish I Knew
I'm A Fool To Want You
Indian Summer
It Ain't Necessarily So

It Never Entered My Mind
It's You Or No One
Just One Of Those Things
Love For Sale
Love Walked In
Lover, Come Back To Me
The Man I Love
Mr. Lucky
My Funny Valentine
My Heart Stood Still
My Man's Gone Now
Old Folks
On A Clear Day
Our Love Is Here To Stay
Secret Love

September In The Rain
Serenade In Blue
Shiny Stockings
Since I Fell For You
So In Love
So Nice (Summer Samba)
Some Other Time
Stormy Weather
The Summer Knows
Summer Night
Summertime
Teach Me Tonight
That Sunday, That Summer
Then I'll Be Tired Of You
There's No You

A Time For Love
Time On My Hands
'Tis Autumn
Where Or When
Who Cares?
With A Song In My Heart
You Go To My Head
Ain't No Sunshine
'Round Midnight
The Girl From Ipanema
Bluesette
And Hundreds More!

The New Real Book - Volume 1 (C, Bb or Eb)

Angel Eyes
Anthropology
Autumn Leaves
Beautiful Love
Bernie's Tune
Blue Bossa
Blue Daniel
But Beautiful
Chain Of Fools
Chelsea Bridge
Compared To What
Darn That Dream
Desafinado
Early Autumn
Eighty One

E.S.P.
Everything Happens To Me
Fall
Feel Like Makin' Love
Footprints
Four
Four On Six
Gee Baby Ain't I Good
To You
Gone With The Wind
Here's That Rainy Day
I Love Lucy
I Mean You
I Should Care
I Thought About You

If I Were A Bell
Imagination
The Island
Jersey Bounce
Joshua
Lady Bird
Like Someone In Love
Line For Lyons
Little Sunflower
Lush Life
Mercy, Mercy, Mercy
The Midnight Sun
Monk's Mood
Moonlight In Vermont
My Shining Hour

Nature Boy
Nefertiti
Nothing Personal
Oleo
Once I Loved
Out Of This World
Pent Up House
Polkadots And Moon-
beams
Portrait Of Tracy
Put It Where You Want It
Robbin's Nest
Ruby, My Dear
Satin Doll
Search For Peace

Shaker Song
Skylark
A Sleepin' Bee
Solar
Speak No Evil
St. Thomas
Street Life
Tenderly
These Foolish Things
This Masquerade
Three Views Of A Secret
Waltz For Debby
Willow Weep For Me
And Many More!

The New Real Book - Volume 2 (C, Bb or Eb)

Afro-Centric
After You've Gone
Along Came Betty
Bessie's Blues
Black Coffee
Blues For Alice
Body And Soul
Bolivia
The Boy Next Door
Bye Bye Blackbird
Cherokee
A Child Is Born
Cold Duck Time
Day By Day

Django
Equinox
Exactly Like You
Falling Grace
Five Hundred Miles High
Freedom Jazz Dance
Giant Steps
Got A Match?
Harlem Nocturne
Hi-Fly
Honeysuckle Rose
I Hadn't Anyone 'Til You
I'll Be Around
I'll Get By

Ill Wind
I'm Glad There Is You
Impressions
In Your Own Sweet Way
It's The Talk Of The Town
Jordu
Killer Joe
Lullaby Of The Leaves
Manha De Carneval
The Masquerade Is Over
Memories Of You
Moment's Notice
Mood Indigo
My Ship

Naima
Nica's Dream
Once In A While
Perdido
Rosetta
Sea Journey
Senor Blues
September Song
Seven Steps To Heaven
Silver's Serenade
So Many Stars
Some Other Blues
Song For My Father
Sophisticated Lady

Spain
Stablemates
Stardust
Sweet And Lovely
That's All
There Is No Greater Love
'Til There Was You
Time Remembered
Turn Out The Stars
Unforgettable
While We're Young
Whisper Not
Will You Still Be Mine?
You're Everything
And Many More!

The New Real Book - Volume 3 (C, Bb, Eb or Bass clef)

Actual Proof
Ain't That Peculiar
Almost Like Being In Love
Another Star
Autumn Serenade
Bird Of Beauty
Black Nile
Blue Moon
Butterfly
Caravan
Ceora
Close Your Eyes
Creepin'
Day Dream
Dolphin Dance

Don't Be That Way
Don't Blame Me
Emily
Everything I Have Is
Yours
For All We Know
Freedomland
The Gentle Rain
Get Ready
A Ghost Of A Chance
Heat Wave
How Sweet It Is
I Fall In Love Too Easily
I Got It Bad

I Hear A Rhapsody
If You Could See Me Now
In A Mellow Tone
In A Sentimental Mood
Inner Urge
Invitation
The Jitterbug Waltz
Just Friends
Just You, Just Me
Knock On Wood
The Lamp Is Low
Laura
Let's Stay Together
Litha
Lonely Woman

Maiden Voyage
Moon And Sand
Moonglow
My Girl
On Green Dolphin Street
Over The Rainbow
Prelude To A Kiss
Respect
Ruby
The Second Time Around
Serenata
The Shadow Of Your Smile
So Near, So Far
Solitude
Speak Like A Child
Spring Is Here

Stairway To The Stars
Star Eyes
Stars Fell On Alabama
Stompin' At The Savoy
Sugar
Sweet Lorraine
Taking A Chance On Love
This Is New
Too High
(Used To Be A) Cha Cha
When Lights Are Low
You Must Believe In Spring
And Many More!

Other Jazz Publications

The Jazz Theory Book

By Mark Levine, the most comprehensive Jazz Theory book ever published! $38 list price.

- Over 500 pages of text and over 750 musical examples.
- Written in the language of the working jazz musician, this book is easy to read and user-friendly. At the same time, it is the most comprehensive study of jazz harmony and theory ever published.
- Mark Levine has worked with Bobby Hutcherson, Cal Tjader, Joe Henderson, Woody Shaw, and many other jazz greats.

The European Real Book

An amazing collection of some of the greatest jazz compositions ever recorded! Available in C, Bb and Eb. $40

- Over 100 of Europe's best jazz writers.
- 100% accurate, composer-approved charts.
- 400 pages of fresh, exciting sounds from virtually every country in Europe.
- Sher Music's superior legibility and signature calligraphy makes reading the music easy.

Listen to FREE MP3 FILES of many of the songs at www.shermusic.com!

The Jazz Piano Book

By Mark Levine, Concord recording artist and pianist with Cal Tjader. For beginning to advanced pianists. The only truly comprehensive method ever published! Over 300 pages. $32

Richie Beirach –"The best new method book available."
Hal Galper – "This is a must!"
Jamey Aebersold – "This is an invaluable resource for any pianist."
James Williams – "One of the most complete anthologies on jazz piano."

Also available in Spanish! ¡El Libro del Jazz Piano!

Concepts For Bass Soloing

By Chuck Sher and Marc Johnson, (bassist with Bill Evans, etc.) The only book ever published that is specifically designed to improve your soloing! $26

- Includes two CDs of Marc Johnson soloing on each exercise
- Transcriptions of bass solos by: Eddie Gomez, John Patitucci, Scott LaFaro, Jimmy Haslip, etc.

"It's a pleasure to encounter a Bass Method so well conceived and executed." – **Steve Swallow**

The Yellowjackets Songbook

Complete package contains six separate spiral-bound books, one each for:

- Piano/partial score • C melody lead sheet
- Synthesizer/miscellaneous parts
- Bb & Eb Horn melody part • Bass • Drums

Contains 20 great tunes from their entire career. Charts exactly as recorded – approved by the Yellowjackets. World famous Sher Music Co. accuracy and legibility. Over 400 pages, $38 list price.

The Improvisor's Bass Method

By Chuck Sher. A complete method for electric or acoustic bass, plus transcribed solos and bass lines by Mingus, Jaco, Ron Carter, Scott LaFaro, Paul Jackson, Ray Brown, and more! Over 200 pages. $16

International Society of Bassists – "Undoubtedly the finest book of its kind."
Eddie Gomez – "Informative, readily comprehensible and highly imaginative"

The World's Greatest Fake Book

Jazz & Fusion Tunes by: **Coltrane, Mingus, Jaco, Chick Corea, Bird, Herbie Hancock, Bill Evans, McCoy, Beirach, Ornette, Wayne Shorter, Zawinul, AND MANY MORE!** $32

Chick Corea – "Great for any students of jazz.'
Dave Liebman – "The fake book of the 80's."
George Cables – "The most carefully conceived fake book I've ever seen."

The Jazz Solos of Chick Corea

Over 150 pages of Chick's greatest solos; "Spain", "Litha", "Windows", "Sicily", etc. for all instrumentalists, single line transcriptions, not full piano score. $18

Chick Corea – "I don't know anyone I would trust more to correctly transcribe my improvisations."

The New Real Book Play-Along CDs (For Volume 1)

CD #1 - Jazz Classics - Lady Bird, Bouncin' With Bud, Up Jumped Spring, Monk's Mood, Doors, Very Early, Eighty One, Voyage **& More!**
CD #2 - Choice Standards - Beautiful Love, Darn That Dream, Moonlight In Vermont, Trieste, My Shining Hour, I Should Care **& More!**
CD #3 - Pop-Fusion - Morning Dance, Nothing Personal, La Samba, Hideaway, This Masquerade, Three Views Of A Secret, Rio **& More!**
World-Class Rhythm Sections, featuring Mark Levine, Larry Dunlap, Sky Evergreen, Bob Magnusson, Keith Jones, Vince Lateano & Tom Hayashi

Recent Sher Music Publications

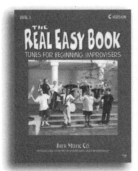

The Real Easy Book Vol. 1
TUNES FOR BEGINNING IMPROVISERS

Published by Sher Music Co. in conjunction with the Stanford Jazz Workshop. $19 list price.

The easiest tunes from Horace Silver, Eddie Harris, Freddie Hubbard, Red Garland, Sonny Rollins, Cedar Walton, Wes Montgomery Cannonball Adderly, etc. Get yourself or your beginning jazz combo sounding good right away with the first fake book ever designed for the beginning improviser.
Available in C, Bb, Eb and Bass Clef.

The Real Easy Book Vol. 2
TUNES FOR INTERMEDIATE IMPROVISERS

Published by Sher Music Co. in conjunction with the Stanford Jazz Workshop. Over 240 pages. $29.

The best intermediate-level tunes by: Charlie Parker, John Coltrane, Miles Davis, John Scofield, Sonny Rollins, Horace Silver, Wes Montgomery, Freddie Hubbard, Cal Tjader, Cannonball Adderly, and more! Both volumes feature instructional material tailored for each tune. Perfect for jazz combos!
Available in C, Bb, Eb and Bass Clef.

The All Jazz Real Book

Over 540 pages of tunes as recorded by: Miles, Trane, Bill Evans, Cannonball, Scofield, Brecker, Yellowjackets, Bird, Mulgrew Miller, Kenny Werner, MJQ, McCoy Tyner, Kurt Elling, Brad Mehldau, Don Grolnick, Kenny Garrett, Patitucci, Jerry Bergonzi, Stanley Clarke, Tom Harrell, Herbie Hancock, Horace Silver, Stan Getz, Sonny Rollins, and MORE!

Includes a free CD of many of the melodies (featuring Bob Sheppard & Friends.). $44 list price.
Available in C, Bb, Eb

The Latin Bass Book
A PRACTICAL GUIDE
By Oscar Stagnaro

The only comprehensive book ever published on how to play bass in authentic Afro-Cuban, Brazilian, Caribbean, Latin Jazz & South American styles.
$34 list price

Over 250 pages of transcriptions of Oscar Stagnaro playing each exercise. Learn from the best!

Includes: 3 Play-Along CDs to accompany each exercise, featuring world-class rhythm sections.

Metaphors For The Musician
By Randy Halberstadt

This practical and enlightening book will help any jazz player or vocalist look at music with "new eyes." Designed for any level of player, on any instrument, "Metaphors For The Musician" provides numerous exercises throughout to help the reader turn these concepts into musical reality.

Guaranteed to help you improve your musicianship. 330 pages - $29 list price. Satisfaction guaranteed!

Inside The Brazilian Rhythm Section
By Nelson Faria and Cliff Korman

This is the first book/CD package ever published that provides an opportunity for bassists, guitarists, pianists and drummers to interact and play-along with a master Brazilian rhythm section. Perfect for practicing both accompanying and soloing.

$28 list price for book and 2 CDs - including the charts for the CD tracks and sample parts for each instrument, transcribed from the recording. Satisfaction guaranteed!

The finest in Jazz & Latin publications
Sher Music Co.
www.shermusic.com

See www.shermusic.com for more information, including a complete list of tunes in all our fake books.
To order, call (800) 444-7437 or fax (707) 763-2038